Secret #5
of Million Dollar
Producers

by
Ken Doyle
and
Lauren Eichner Doyle

Secret #5 of Million Dollar Producers

Published by Getting Results Coaching
Sarasota, FL

Table of Contents

The Fifth Secret

What is it that makes 'that guy' a Million-Dollar Producer? Is he special in some way? Does he have some unique talent or trait? Why can one guy reach a million dollars in production in just seven years, while many spend 30 years in their careers and never reach it? How can one woman do over a million dollars in production working just 20 hours per week, while you work 60 hours and still have not touched the golden level? And, what the heck is it about the producer who does six million per year or has an astounding billion (yes, with a 'B') dollars in assets under management?

We have been coaching producers like these for nearly two decades and have a keen understanding of what sets them apart from the rest of the crowd in the industry. The answer is both simple, yet complex at the same time. It is complex because there is not one single trait or ability that makes the distinction. But it is simple because this one key, the fifth secret, is what lends nearly all of them the ability to put into practice the other four secrets. Without the fifth secret, the chance of reaching a million dollars in production is nearly impossible.

You see, we all would like a quick fix, a simple solution and easy strategy. What this group of producers recognizes is that it is not always that simple. The fifth secret requires an ongoing commitment to being excellent, to being the best. They recognize that in order to make the top grade in the business, they need to be a student of not only the business but of themselves. Ahhh, we have finally gotten to the fifth secret. While most advisors spend much of their time studying the latest investment strategies or the sexiest best practice of the day, Million Dollar Advisors do those things as well, but they also become a student of themselves.

What exactly does that mean?

It means that they learn more about themselves and others than the rest of financial advisors. They study the psychology of the sale, the psychology of relationships, and most importantly, the psychology of themselves. The good news is that you have illustrated that you, too, recognize that there is more to being highly successful in financial services than searching for the latest 'pill' to take or best practice to follow. Don't get me wrong, best practices, training programs and marketing strategies are all important. They can improve an advisor's performance and increase business. But I want you to think of how many marketing strategies you've tried, best practices you have deployed and books you have read. It is probably a lot, and yet you are still reaching for the golden ticket of attaining a million dollars in production.

Perhaps, it is not that those things aren't effective, but maybe it is the person or machine operating them that lacks effectiveness. Tiger Woods is one of the most coached golfers in the profession. He knows how to swing the club. He can accurately putt the ball. All of that thanks to his golfing coaches. But if you sat down with him and asked him what makes him different, he would tell you that what has truly made him one of the greatest golfers of our time is that he became a student of his own mind. His mind was coached as much (if not more) than his golf swing. Having a mind that has been coached makes all of the techniques and skills more effective.

The fifth secret is to work on your own mental game before you can use any business strategy to its greatest effectiveness. There are too many opportunities for your mind to get in the way of employing the best 'best practice' you learn. Just look at the many activities you failed to follow through on for one reason or another. Your mind likely came up with a number of excuses as to why you stopped or never started them. You were too busy. It didn't work. Or the next best thing (or what seemed like the 'easier pill') came along. Your practice is probably full of examples where you lacked the necessary follow through. But instead of employing Secret #5, you looked for the next idea or strategy only to waste more time and money.

You may now be wondering, '"How do I work on my mental game?'

Aha grasshopper, that is what this book is meant to introduce you to and guide you on. You see, when we started this book, the object was to provide you with a number of insights from a myriad of successful advisors from all walks of life. All of these advisors were or are clients of Getting Results Coaching. They include men and women. Young producers and seasoned producers. They are from all over the country from Maine to Hawaii, from the North to the South. They include independent Advisors and Advisors who work in the largest wirehouses.

Each of their stories presents a different frustration or challenge they experienced in the business. You should be able to find yourself in one or more of their stories. They all were asked open-ended questions as to what it was about their coaching experience that made them so successful. It is important to understand that as a coaching firm for Financial Advisors, we incorporate a lot of best practices and even have a trademarked program that employs the 64/4 rule, where 64% of revenue comes from just 4% of clients (think 80/20 Rule squared). They learn to identify, cultivate and replicate the top four percent (and up to the top 20%) of their book of business. Yet, despite all of the useful tools we give them to grow their businesses, just about every one of their responses pointed to a particular principle they learned through their coaching experience with us. It is important for you to have a little background on Getting Results Coaching to understand why these results are so exciting. First off, we have the highest retention rate of nearly any coaching firm in the business. The reason for this is that our work is not close-ended and significant results continue year after year. Top producers understand the need to have a coach on their team to hold them accountable and to keep their vision alive. Each uses their coach to help keep them on top of their mental game as well. Our coaches always recognize each producer's potential, and when the mind starts to make excuses or run astray, it is the coaches' jobs to keep them on track.

So, while each advisor interviewed had the opportunity to express their story any way they chose to, they all had pointed to various principles they learned and employed throughout their coaching as their key to success. We use a principle-based approach to coach our clients. This approach lends itself to longer lasting results and results that reverberate through all areas of their lives, not just in their businesses. This is the key to Secret #5: working on your mental game.

The first iteration of this book simply includes different stories from various advisors. See if you can pull out the various principles from each story that had a great impact on their success. The next version of the book will include a deeper explanation of each of these principles, so you can gain a deeper understanding of each one.

Looking for a quick fix, a single best practice or the latest pill to swallow will only impair your progress. Being truly committed to your success requires a mature understanding that the greatest asset and tool to sharpen is the one between your ears, not just with more knowledge to manipulate the outside world but to manage your internal world.

Should you choose to embark on this adventure, I guarantee you that the rewards will be far reaching. In many of the stories, you will read how the benefits of their coaching process extended far beyond their businesses. Not only will your business grow exponentially, your relationships with your spouse, kids, family and friends will become richer. You will find your life experiences will be grander and more interesting. After all, isn't that what this journey is all about?

So if you have found yourself bored or frustrated with your business, this book is for you. Read on!

Overcoming a Plateau

There's a little secret that was once known only by a few of the most elite in business that is becoming more mainstream. It is the tremendous crossover benefits and advantages that so many financial advisors are reaping as a result of using a business coach.

From Little League to the Olympic Games, coaches are everywhere. You've seen them on the sidelines during events encouraging, cajoling, and occasionally reproaching.

It's no surprise that a seven-year-old playing baseball for the first time needs a coach. At that point, everything is new; everything must be learned: how to hold the bat, when to swing, how to catch, when to advance to the next base to avoid the out. You know, all of the basic skills. It may seem surprising that athletes who have reached the pinnacle of their sports, vying to be the best in the world and take home the Olympic gold medal, continue to use coaches. You'd think at that level, they've learned it all.

However, even at that extraordinary level, coaching remains invaluable. Although these athletes are no longer on the steep learning curve of the seven-year-old, there is still knowledge to be gained, technique to be honed. And maybe even more importantly, there's the accountability factor. Some are self-disciplined enough to rise well before dawn every day to practice and train, but reporting to a coach clearly improves that likelihood across the board, and nothing is achieved without practice.

Imagine taking your career to the next level. What is it you would like to achieve? What are your goals and desires? Like the stories of the individuals that follow, your aspirations can become reality. You are in a profession where there is no limit to the amount of income you can make, yet you have witnessed other producers get complacent and flat line their business. Your profession also allows you to design your business so that it works for you, but many don't take advantage of this benefit.

In this book, we've compiled the stories of many people who faced incredible challenges or realized they'd stagnated in their careers and their businesses. They all had dreams of achieving more both in their professional and personal lives. In their own words, they've openly shared what they faced and what coaching lessons and principles helped them develop and implement solutions and reach success – success that many of them initially deemed impossible.

Some of these individuals were reluctant to seek the guidance of a coach but were inspired by seeing the results that someone they knew achieved through the process.

Chances are you'll see parallels in some of their stories to your own career and life. Maybe you're at a crossroads, facing what seems to be an insurmountable hurdle, or feeling plateaued and uncertain how to realize growth again. Quite possibly, you'll also see parallels in your own aspirations and goals.

Ultimately, it is our hope that you see a little of yourself in some of these individuals. Hopefully, you will gain the insight and confidence to take your own leap of sorts to start your own path or journey to stop 'thinking' about what you would 'like to do someday' and start taking the effective action to realizing those aspirations.

Your dream of success can be a motivator, and when that dream is paired with a knowledgeable coach, astonishing things can happen.

Ken Doyle and Lauren Eichner-Doyle
Getting Results Coaching

Chapter 1

Double Production Effectively

S ome days are great; some days aren't. Are the ebbs and tides controlling your outlook? Are you feeling great one day only to be knocked down the next? Riding high on a wave only to be dragged back out to sea again, struggling to find the next great wave? Those emotional roller coaster fluctuations are nauseating for most people. Maybe the only thing worse is stagnation.

Stagnation was Ian's frustration. He felt stuck; the business was stagnant. He knew he wanted to do something different and was looking for innovative ideas rather than doing the same thing over and over.

"There were a lot of ebbs and tides in my mood," Ian says. "I'd feel really productive on some days and less so on others. If the cash register was ringing, I was in a good mood; if it wasn't, I was in a bad mood. The coaching process helped shift my thinking because it helped me look at the business as the owner, not an employee. I'm thinking more strategically and less concerned with the day-to-day. With global thinking, the machinations of any given day have less effect on me because I can stay focused on the bigger picture."

For Ian, coaching with Ken Doyle of Getting Results Coaching is as much about life coaching as it is about business coaching. He's gleaned a lot from coaching that he can point to as beneficial in his business as well as his life. For example, he's now very involved in yoga, which is a great outlet for him and improves his consciousness about his diet and overall health. That's been another shift in his thinking.

The coaching process also helped him double his asset base and subsequently more than double his income. The business didn't simply grow – it grew effectively.

Ian explains, "We attract clients for a reason now, and those relationships are far stronger than the ones we created by cold calling. My goal isn't to be the cheapest but to be the best. If you're focused on price alone, rather than value, at some point you won't do well because you won't be the cheapest. We focus on quality and service and deal with people who appreciate that."

Through coaching, Ian learned to differentiate relationships with clients. He recalls being very afraid not to retain everyone, but now focuses on the quality of the relationship rather than the size of the account. Relationships matter to him more than the account's daily market value. By culling relationships that were non-productive, Ian saw that it freed up space to bring in better and deeper ones. He didn't keep clients who weren't good relationships, and he doesn't take them on now from the start.

> "We attract clients for a reason now, and those relationships are far stronger than the ones we created by cold calling."
> ~Ian A.

Deeper relationships are a foundation. Ian's had clients through the "tech debacle" of the 90's and through the '08-

'09 recession and is proud of the fact that all of his clients have more assets and positive returns. He's also proud of being voted to New Jersey Monthly as a top advisor for the second consecutive year.

Although not one for small talk, Ian describes his client relationships: "During Hurricane Sandy, my clients were actually calling me to see if I was okay. Plus I've had many clients ask me to manage money for their kids after they're gone. They don't want the money going into just anyone's hands. They appreciate what I do, and that's a great, great compliment."

There's also a big difference between a champion and a client. Even good clients may never be champions. The champions will walk through fire for you, love you, bring other champions to your business, and make your work not feel like work. Getting Results revealed a process to cultivate champions to Ian and held him accountable to working the process. Many financial advisors fail to develop first class cabins of their business because no one holds them to account for doing the actual work. Building solid relationships takes time, attention and effort.

Ian has been a huge proponent of coaching: "I've referred Ken to many people who also hired him. I'm pleased by that because the broader the community of like-minded people, the better off we all are. There's a lot of cross-pollination and idea sharing as a result. Some coaching calls may not always feel productive, but then there's an epiphany... an a-ha moment... and that one call is suddenly worth a whole year of calls. A coach is a sounding board, and it's great to have someone outside your office who's not your manager whose job it is to make sure you're sitting at your desk working all day. It's great to have another perspective."

The longer you stay in the conversation of building a business by design, the greater the probability that it will happen. Although you may not feel a coaching call is productive at that particular time, the thoughts and ideas are coalescing. It takes time for rice to cook but if you put out the flame, the effort is thwarted.

Not everyone is open to coaching. Everyone says they want results, but they're either not coachable or not serious about it. Ian likens those folks to people who want to lose weight but don't want to diet or people who want to exercise but don't want to go to the gym.

He concludes, "The best of the best use coaches, whether you're a golfer or an athlete or in business. There are things a coach can do for you that you're probably not thinking of yourself. The process gives you another set of eyes and ears. Maybe it's a suggestion to try this or try that. You shift something that you wouldn't think to shift. It gets you away from not seeing the forest for the trees."

What are you seeing in your life and your career: the forest or the trees? If you're continuing to focus on the trees, it's time to shift your perspective and your thinking. If you're tired of your moods being affected by the ebbs and tides, it's time to get off the roller coaster. If you're stagnating, it's time to shake things up.

Chapter 2

Held Hostage

A good juggler is fun to watch, especially when they continue to add more balls to the equation… or swords or flaming batons. The problem is most of us can't juggle, either literally or figuratively. Sure, you're probably working to keep a few balls in the air, and maybe you're managing the process adequately. Or maybe you're very nervous about what happens next if someone tosses you just one more ball (let alone a sword or something aflame) or worse, you lose your concentration for a split second. The result: Everything comes crashing down. Catastrophe is only one mishandled ball away.

Brenda admits she had too many balls in the air, and her result was a lack of focus. Upon a colleague's suggestion, she sought out a coach. "I felt like I needed more efficiency and organization and that I was going about the business the wrong way," Brenda says. "Suddenly I was working in a vacuum and knew I needed a more purposeful track."

Everything was gang-busters until '08. She went from bringing assets in quickly, almost too quickly, to a sudden slowdown. The magnitude of how bad the markets could be hit her like a brick truck. Brenda admits not being super efficient, even messy, and didn't blueprint her processes very well. She felt down and discouraged, constantly overwhelmed and hated walking into her office, which was in her own home.

"When Ken of Getting Results was recommended to me, I didn't have the courage to call at the time," continues Brenda. "My son, who was thinking of going into business with me at the time, recommended another group coaching program. Their focus was the bottom line and getting more assets under management. That wasn't where I wanted to focus, and their process made me nauseous just thinking about it. I didn't need 'more.' I needed the right focus on the right things."

On the other hand, Ken's approach was to fix herself first before trying to fix her business. She had not been good at separating life and work, a problem compounded by the fact that she works from home. Her lack of focus and organization was also plaguing her personal life. That's not surprising since we are all singular individuals. The person you are in the office is the person you are at home and vice versa. Brenda felt as if her coach held the bridge that she needed to cross over that abyss.

Through coaching, Brenda learned what to say to help people tackle their issues and to handle any push back by pushing back herself. She developed the courage she needed to take the risk of losing a client – one client in particular who created a stabbing pain... when she wasn't merely a huge, constant knot in the stomach. Brenda describes it: "I had one tortuous client, and I learned that I needed to get her out of my life and how to do it. Ken told me to hang up and do it, then call him back. The result? Freedom. Total freedom. I suddenly felt like I had been a P.O.W and after that call, it was like the American troops had stormed in and freed me. Not a week has gone by that I'm not thankful for that. Through coaching, I learned that I am worth it and carry that attitude with me."

Her quality of life has improved as a result of the coaching process. As a solo adviser, Brenda describes herself as the "chief coffee fetcher, head honcho and chief compliance officer" all rolled into one. With full responsibility for her business, she always had trouble breaking away. Until this year. With a leap of faith, she finally took a long-overdue vacation, traveling to Turkey.

"It was an out-of-the-box trip for me," Brenda explains. "I'm not a risk taker, and for me, this was very unconventional. But it cemented the fact that I really needed to replenish myself, so I don't become overwhelmed. I find myself working a lot less on evenings and weekends. Now I encourage myself not to walk into the office after hours. I'm working fewer hours... appropriately." Her coach provided the extra support and borrowed confidence to take certain leaps she ordinarily would not have.

Learning to balance her personal and professional life has been one of the biggest benefits, and Brenda sees now how sorely it was needed. Also getting rid of inappropriate clients has been pivotal. She longer feels like that P.O.W. being held captive by clients who aren't beneficial to her. She no longer hates walking into her own home office.

> "I don't have to grade myself. If I put my all into something and it doesn't pan out, it's not my fault."
> ~ Brenda

One of the toughest concepts for her to get her arms around was the idea of being committed to the outcome but unattached to the results. "I now understand how that rings true for me," Brenda says. "I don't have to grade myself. If I put my all into something and it doesn't pan out, it's not my fault. The universe doesn't always go your way. I've also applied that in my personal life as well. When there are things I want to happen, I work hard to get them, but if they don't occur, I no longer personalize it the way I did."

Are you being held hostage? Either by clients who aren't benefitting you or by your own preconceived notions? Maybe disorganization and the lack of an organized approach are the chains that hold you. Or maybe your attempt to separate your personal and professional selves, an inherently impossible task, is holding you hostage. Like Brenda, would you like to appreciate the feeling of being freed from that – for good? You have the power to free yourself. You don't need storm troopers to swoop in and save you. With the right coaching, you can unlock whatever is holding you back.

Chapter 3

Staying in the Game

Do you run your day or does your day run you? It's a common problem. You show up at work and things seem to spin out of control within minutes. Before you know it, it's lunch, and by the next time you turn around, it's 5:00 and you've made little, if any, forward progress. The next thing you know you've hit another Friday, another end of month, another end of quarter, and don't look now, but the holidays and a new year are right around the corner. Didn't we just celebrate that? Running on that treadmill is what happens when you can't control your day. It takes you out of the game.

That was Randy's biggest concern. His day ran him rather than the other way around. When you show up at the office and are out of control, it's frustrating, irritating and puts you in a bad mood. Nobody likes to always be doing what they don't want to do in the first place, and that's exactly what happens when you're not in charge of your day. You're stuck doing what you don't want to do.

So Randy turned to Ken of Getting Results. A few things resonated with him right off the bat: "He said that your business is a lot like a dog. If you don't train it, it does what it wants and you're left to clean up the mess. I laughed at the analogy because we'd just gotten a dog, and it had the run of the house when we were gone. And since puppies do what puppies do, we'd come home to a mess – chewed shoes and accidents to clean up. Our vet told us about confining the puppy when we left the house to gain control, and I saw the business correlation as soon as Ken mentioned it. I had to control my business just like controlling the puppy."

Through coaching, Randy's come a long way in taking control of his day. He's identified the most productive part of his day and schedules his client calls then. He's also learned to segment his day into blocks, not unlike confining his puppy when he leaves the house. Now he returns similar calls within the same block of time, so he can stay on track rather than starting, stopping and re-setting. For Randy that wasn't as easy as it sounds.

> **"Knowing my elite clients makes me so much more aware of opportunities to further my relationship with them."**
> **~ Randy B.**

"I wanted to tackle every issue as soon as it came up," Randy says, "but that wasn't productive for me or my clients. Plus we have a tendency to think we're way more important than we are. Whenever the phone rang, I was convinced that people needed to talk to me right then. Ken once asked me if I thought my clients were thinking about me when they got up in the morning and poured the milk on their cereal. Of course not. I realized then that I had to get over myself. I could do a better job for my clients when I was most productive, not necessarily at the moment they called."

When you understand the distinction between being busy and being productive, you retake ownership of your daily calendar.

Client list reduction resulted from the same thinking. By reducing his client list by 25 percent, Randy can better serve his remaining clients. Again, that didn't come without a struggle. He didn't want to give away clients. Plus Randy learned to segment those that remained into classes, like first-class on an airplane. Those in first class get better treatment, bigger seats and more leg room. It's what they pay for. Passengers in coach don't get the perks, and Randy realized that they don't expect them because they know they didn't pay for them. It's a choice to accept lesser service for a lower rate. His clients are the same.

Randy continues, "Knowing my elite clients makes me so much more aware of opportunities to further my relationship with them. Before, if one of them mentioned becoming a grandparent, I'd congratulate them. Now I congratulate them and expand the conversation to delve into what we can do to help them with this life change and new milestone. It wows them, and now I can deliver that type of service regularly." This was the direct result of working The Champion Path™.

Business is like playing a game that can never be won. It can only be played. The key is to always be playing. That was a surprising concept for Randy and one he's taken to heart. He realized that he had a habit of taking himself out of the game. Being mad, upset, unproductive or lazy always takes you off the playing field.

"I never realized how often I wasn't on the field of play," explains Randy. "I wasn't as engaged as I should have been. Plus I had a habit of creating drama where none existed. For example, if a client moved money and then didn't return my call, I convinced myself that he was angry with me or moved to another adviser. In reality, he'd been out of town and had a logical need for the money movement. Meanwhile, I spent a few days off the field of play worrying about the situation. Now I'm much more engaged even though I'm a lot busier."

A good coach challenges you and takes you to another level while some coaches take your money and tell you what you want to hear. Learning to take feedback and applying it to make improvements to stay in the game is a critical component for success.

Are you staying in the game? Or do comments from others, distractions and negativity keep you on the sidelines. The game can't be won; it can only be played. If you want to move forward in your career and your life, you have to stay on the playing field.

Chapter 4

"He Gave Away 100% of My Income"

You have a monthly income, and no doubt, you have monthly expenses for which you've budgeted and created a balance sheet: mortgage, utilities, food, transportation, entertainment, clothing, retirement savings, and the list goes on. You probably feel stressed when your monthly expenses occasionally exceed your income. Maybe you tap into your savings account or use your credit card harder. A lopsided balance sheet creates angst for most people. What would you do if your monthly income suddenly dropped to zero? Through no fault of your own? Zero. Now what?

That's exactly what happened to Jason. In the middle of a messy divorce and custody battle, the judge misinterpreted gross and net income and awarded his soon-to-be ex-wife 100 percent of his after tax income. All of it. And the judge would not listen to Jason pointing out his math error. Jason later appealed, and the judge denied it.

Jason recalls the original ruling occurred on a Friday. He was out of his mind and freaking out. With the stroke of a judge's pen, he literally had no income to cover his own living expenses. It had all been given away in the form of alimony and child support because of a math error. Friday night was horrible. Jason called his coach, Ken Doyle of Getting Results Coaching. Ken's comment was, "Let's figure this out."

Ken helped him cut through the drama that had hijacked Jason's mind. Jason believed that this was an end of the world event. No doubt it was a bad event but not an end of the world event. Jason was in panic mode, so like all of us when we are under a tremendous amount of stress, we can make dumb decisions. Stress does not make us smarter, it makes us stupid. So Ken asked him a simple question: "Now what? Are you going to roll over and die?" Jason said he was not going to die... so figure it out.

They talked, and Saturday was a little better. Sunday was more normal, and by Monday, Jason was super charged and knew he could figure out what three days earlier was a disastrous event. He broke into his IRA and savings and continued to sharpen his focus to work smarter and more efficiently. His business has doubled. While he likes to think he had something to do with that improvement, he also admits that he probably couldn't have done it without a coach.

He began the coaching process at a time in his life when there were too many distractions in his way. The hostile divorce and custody battle led to stress that made him so sick, he was hospitalized.

"I knew that a journey of 1,000 miles begins with a single step," Jason explains, "but there are a helluva lot of steps in 1,000 miles. Ken helped me understand that changing my life couldn't happen overnight because I didn't get to where I was overnight. The point was really driven home to me when I was moving. I had all these boxes in the storage unit and was trying to decide which one to pick up to start moving. Looked at one, too big. Looked at a second, too small. I was literally turning in circles trying to decide which box to move, when the voice in my head shouted, 'Just grab one! It doesn't matter, you have to move them all.' That was really a defining moment in my metamorphosis."

Jason learned that you can't play the game effectively when the field is full of razor wire. You have to clear the field of the obstacles you face first, and there was no shortage of obstacles for Jason. His biggest one was the divorce and custody battle, and that created distractions and ongoing loss of momentum. He learned to stop worrying about things beyond his control. Through the coaching work he's done, Jason has adopted a don't-take-anything-personally mantra.

He continues, "I laugh more often than I ever have because it's not personal, and I learned not to take it personally. Negative things that anyone says about me define them, not me. When I look back, I used to take responsibility for things I had not done or that I had no control over. It's incredible to me how I used to begrudge, accept or worry about that which I can't control. I'm a far different man today than when I started working with Ken, and I continue the work. There's a thrill and pleasure for me in continuing to evolve. And I hope to be an even better and more aware person a year from now and the years after that."

> "Negative things that anyone says about me define them, not me."
> ~ Jason R.

One of the biggest surprises for Jason in his coaching results was not how easy it is to change because it's not, but how he shackled himself into interpreting certain things as impossible. He never imagined himself being a million-dollar producer; he thought it was impossible. But he's achieved it for two years in a row. Jason now embraces the "go figure" concept. He now understands that everything he wants to accomplish is a probability. All he has to do is figure out how to make it a reality. He infers the phrase "go figure" very positively now and understands game planning.

"I know I can overcome anything. I have complete awareness now. As soon as I realize I'm off the path, I'm immediately back on the path and moving forward. 'Committed to the outcome; unattached to the result' has meaning for me. For example, I'm committed to reducing alimony, but if I lose, I lose. I can walk away knowing I gave it my best shot. I'm happier than ever, and I know I can be happier still."

Jason continues the coaching process and recommends it to everyone he knows. He's seen the overwhelming return on investment in terms of both success and happiness. He now has plenty of experience clearing obstacles off the field. He overcame a 100 percent loss of income. What obstacles are you facing that you need to clear off the field? How are you reacting to adversity? While your obstacles may not seem as extraordinary as Jason's, they are keeping you out of the game and thwarting your forward progress. Imagine how much better your own life can be without the obstacles. Imagine realizing that nothing is impossible.

Chapter 5

More with Less

Time is like a jar of helium – it fills the container it's in. Most of us excel at wasting time. Most of us are very good at filling that jar and letting it expand with useless things. Sure, we convince ourselves that we are busy beyond belief and that there's no way we could fit another task into our already overfilled days. Is there too much on your plate or are you trying to keep too many plates in the air? Busy and productive are not the same. Being busy on the wrong tasks is too often the baloney that we convince ourselves is productivity. That's what Tim learned, and he also learned that with the right process you can easily get more done in less time.

Tim's frustration was founded in being in the same business and the same location for twelve years, struggling to grow that business organically. Day after day, year after year, he faced the same challenges over and over. It was like being on a treadmill – constantly moving but going nowhere. He felt they were doing wonderful work for happy clients but were unable to convert that into new clients or referrals. Over the years, he'd also attended a lot of sales coaching and presentation training workshops, but until he started working with Getting Results Coaching, nothing truly touched on the big picture.

"Business and personal lives affect each other," he says, "and I had long made the mistake of trying to keep them separate. You know the old saying about doing the same thing over and expecting different results is the definition of insanity? Through the coaching process,

I became accountable to get out of that cycle and learned to live by design rather than by default."

As the sales manager, Tim also learned the importance of process. In investment management, you can't tell what the environment will be, so you can only control that which you can actually control, and that's sales activity. According to Tim, Ken lives the process he teaches. He sets meeting times and expectations and meets them on the nose, so Tim began emulating that approach and implementing those qualities in his own business.

Tim continues, "Don't miss meetings and don't waste other people's time has become our mantra. In this business, our time is everything, so by setting up processes, we've eliminated the unproductive parts of our day and can concentrate on the work that has real impact." Additionally, Tim discovered that by organizing the time he spent on the sales process, he had more time to spend on research and with clients – the most valuable things he can do in a day. In eight months, they've garnered real results, and the process has set him free.

> **"Through the coaching process, I learned to live by design rather than by default."**
> **~ Tim L.**

Giving staff measurable goals and reminding them of those goals eliminated all subjectivity from relationships in the office. Tim's role in the office is improved, and he can now separate his role as the boss from that of friend. He explains, "Now I can say, 'I like you as a person, and I mean that, but you've only had seven meetings. How do we get you to ten?' Metrics and measurements are the key to that."

Success is based on sales effort, and now that they've finished the organization of the sales effort, the firm is seeing much more sales activity. Plus by moving the team to structured process, Tim and his partner are guaranteeing profitability which then falls to him on the bottom line. The simple lesson learned is that activity drives production. Give your attention to activity, and production will follow. Make sure activity and production targets are defined. The more important of the two is activity.

Of course, quality of life goes beyond the bottom line. Tim states, "Self-determination is a powerful force, so feeling in control of that which you can and should control has a huge impact on quality of life. Enjoyment? Totally. And I sleep at night."

As a business owner, Tim has appreciated having a coach hold him accountable for his actions. The extra set of eyes has been a benefit, and his coach typically doesn't pull any punches. It's an attribute that Tim knows has helped them improve their business. "The best part of the relationship," Tim says, "is that Ken strips away all that baloney we force ourselves to believe to get to what we actually need to do to succeed."

How much baloney is in your life? How many plates are you trying to keep in the air? By managing yourself, you become more effective and get more done. Could you use more time? The answer lies in doing more with less which is about finding what your particular leverage points are.

Chapter 6

At a Crossroads

What is success? Is it to be well thought of in the eyes of your peers and doing what everybody else is doing? Maybe. Or is success creating your own path and your own business such that is a reflection of your values, goals and beliefs. The mediocre conform; the great choose their own path.

We each face crossroads in our lives. The decision to turn in one direction or another affects what happens next and sometimes sets a firm course for your life. We've all probably stood at that intersection, trying to look in each direction as far as we can to view the landscape before taking a step. What if I choose the wrong path? What if I can't turn around? What if I get lost? Worry about turning the wrong direction can be both debilitating and paralyzing. Some folks become so paralyzed, they never move forward, frozen in the crossroads.

Gregg was at such a crossroad. When he started in the financial industry, he thought that being cut throat was the personality trait you needed to succeed. He saw that the aggressors were the ones seeming to enjoy monetary success. Being aggressive and tenacious, he thought, was the path he needed to be on. There was only one problem – that wasn't who he was. It was also about the time he began his relationship with Getting Results Coaching.

"Now when I look back at that crossroad moment," Gregg explains, "I realize just how ludicrous it was. 'Cut throat' wasn't who I was. There aren't two of me. The ingredients that make up the professional and the personal side of my life are the same."

Through the coaching process, he quickly realized that there is complete overlap between his personal and professional lives. If someone is aggressive and overly competitive in the office, that same person is not going to be soft and easy-going at home. The question to answer is: Who do you intend to be? It's equally important to be cognizant of the answer to that question at all times to create a seamless transition from work to home and vice versa. So who do you intend to be?

Gregg realized that the nature of his business did not have to preclude that crossover. He admitted that when he started, the criterion for client selection was along the lines of "heartbeat and checkbook." Self described as marginally successful when he began the coaching process, the biggest shift for him was realizing that he could choose who he wanted to do business with.

"I pay more attention to my business relationships now more than ever before," Gregg continues. "It has to be good for you and for me. If there's no affinity, I don't pursue the relationship. My clients are also my friends.

"I'm wealthier than I was when I started talking to Ken, but it's not necessarily cause and effect because on the day I met him, I was wealthier than the day before that. However, it's far less stressful now, and I can directly attribute that to my work with Getting Results."

Gregg struggled to overcome insecurity and internal fear. He thought that working with a coach would make those insecurities magically disappear, but it turned out that they never disappear. Success lies in managing them. Appearance of calm is mastering the trade.

He continues, "The last thing you would describe me as is insecure; however, it's the first way I would describe myself. The difference is that I can now manage those emotions."

Great athletes all have coaches. Athletes who aspire to greatness have coaches. A coach helps uncover and nurture the tremendous potential that exists within each of us. A coach can be the catalyst to help anyone see what is possible rather than being stuck in embracing only that which seems impossible. A coach can help you move out of the crossroads and make real progress. That's what Gregg discovered.

Now he's surprised that after 21 years in the business that he still sees so much potential. He's as excited today about what he does than he was when he started. In fact, he's even more excited because the ceiling is so much higher now than he realized it could be.

> "If there's no affinity, I don't pursue the relationship. My clients are also my friends."
> ~ Gregg A.

The weekly interaction forces him to stop the clock and take time away from the daily minutiae of the day – the minutiae in which we all get so caught up. He explains that it gives him time to have a completely different perspective by looking down the road five or ten years and continually re-focus on the big picture.

Gregg concludes, "Now I see that I am responsible for everything I do, and that's a very liberating feeling. When you understand that you can take responsibility for every outcome and when your self-awareness is in the right place, you can have a great life. My life is great."

Where are you in relation to crossroads in your life? Do you know which way to turn? Find a guide who has helped others design fulfilling businesses; that choice may be hard, but it will be the most rewarding.

Chapter 7

Save the Drama for the Stage

Office politics. A lot of people will quickly roll their eyes when they hear the phrase and insist they despise them. However, many of those same people are just as quick to become willing participants in the game, probably without realizing the role they play. Sometimes it's founded in the company culture or even in someone's upbringing. Regardless, the end result is the same – a negative energy drain. Office politics is a manifestation of drama that is addictive and time consuming. It is a waste of energy and attention that could be otherwise allocated to productive activities.

Comment, overreaction, jump down someone's throat. That seemed to be the typical way Stacey handled office politics. Drama could be found everywhere, and if it couldn't be found, it wasn't that hard to create. Drama that occurs anywhere but onstage is negative and draining. She didn't realize the extent to which participating in drama, pouncing and blowing things out of proportion kept her from being set free. Then she began working with Ken and Getting Results Coaching.

"Before I began the coaching process," she says with a hearty laugh, "I was amazing... I knew everything!" She admits that her impetus to begin working with a coach was because of her business partner. "He'd gone through some real traumas, and his focus was and still is amazing. I probably wouldn't have hired a coach on my own, but I have never, ever looked back on that decision. In fact, when I first spoke to Ken, I was pushing to get the show on the road and write the check. He continued to push back to learn what Stacey had to work on. I was already learning on my first phone call."

Stacey learned the importance of a number of tenets, but the one that sticks out for her is: Desire the good of all and the universe works with you. She learned not to be part of the drama and gossip both in and out of the office. She went from being a victim, blaming failures and problems on others, to being fully responsible for her own outcomes. As a financial advisor, she knows that if she's not on the phone or networking, she's not going to drive business, and she now knows she is fully and solely responsible for that.

"There's nobody to blame but yourself," continues Stacey. "I went from victim to responsible, and once I got away from the 'woe is me' victim mentality, it truly set me free. Now when I hear that attitude from others, I realize how much better off I am without it."

> "Once I got away from the 'woe is me' victim mentality, it truly set me free."
> ~ Stacy R.

In conjunction with the idea of desiring the good of all, comes what she jokingly refers to as "fairy dust." Stacey conscientiously works to find the positive in everything. While she's always had the innate ability to walk into a room and get everyone talking, she's noticed that now people want to be with her more. The negativity is gone. "Desire the good of all and the universe works with you" is clearly at work.

Two charities, one that provides grants to empower women and girls and the other that helps provide school supplies for underserved children, are now also the beneficiaries of Stacey's fairy dust. She explains, "Embracing 'desiring the good' has helped me tremendously. The charity work has allowed me to create many conversations, and now I'm not just asking for business, I'm having a conversation with people and enjoying being with like-minded people." The business naturally follows.

A second tenet she now embraces (and one of a few that she has posted on her wall) is that whatever you pay attention to you get more of. If you pay attention to drama, you get more drama, and she's glad to be free of that now. Moreover, her production has doubled and she's had the best year of her career.

In addition to improving productivity, Stacey credits the coaching process for two very vital life improvements: exercise and learning. She already enjoyed cycling, but Ken helped her stretch her limits. Now she can boast completion of a 5K race and "tough mudder" challenge as on her list of accomplishments. However, it's not simply about the physical accomplishment, it's about ongoing good health. A motivated mind needs a healthy body to support it.

One of the reasons Getting Results will have its clients embrace physical challenges is because it builds self esteem and confidence. Training for endurance events also provides insights into building a successful financial services practice or any business, for that matter. At first, running seemed impossible to Stacey (much like becoming a $750,000 producer), but running, like production, is broken down into steps. You have a training program to follow, and you will finish the 5k. If you are committed to becoming a $750,000 producer and you follow the program, you will become one. Endurance events and business are the same: Know where the finish line is, commit to your training and just keep moving your feet, and you will cross the finish line!

Always open to learning, Stacey refers to herself as a "culture vulture." She explains, "I'm now doing more like cooking classes, lectures, museum visits and that list goes on and on. Those things make me think, keep me vibrant and young. When you're learning, you're evolving. Honestly, probably the best gifts I got from coaching are exercising and learning. Ken challenged me to be better physically and mentally." Another side benefit of being a vulture of culture is that it keeps her prospecting and meeting people that share a common interest.

Add giving up the drama to Stacy's list as well. If you dislike office politics, don't play a part in them. How much drama is in your life? Unless you're an actor, less is definitely more. Imagine what you would do with all that energy that is swallowed by the drama if you applied it to your business instead. Drama can also occur at home, and that also steals from your business and your life.

Chapter 8

Leadership Has Its Price

If you sit in the corner office, you're well aware of interruptions and the amount of time that goes out the window because of them. Even if you sit in a cubicle, interruptions are a time suck. They keep you from getting to the important tasks that are on your to-do list. They're frustrating. You look around at the end of the day at the pile of work that still has to be done, wondering where the day went. When piled on top of each other, interruptions can stop you dead in your tracks. It's impossible to reach your goals when you're stopped dead. You want to throw up your hands and scream.

Scott didn't actually throw up his hands or scream, but he quickly learned the frustration of interruptions when he took over the business he now runs. He explains, "When you work for someone else, your schedule and tasks are predetermined, but when you take on the leadership role, it's up to you to set your agenda. I felt like my schedule was setting my agenda rather than the other way around. It was very frustrating because I felt like I wasn't doing what needed to be done and certainly wasn't moving forward as quickly as I would like."

Before selecting Ken of Getting Results, Scott interviewed other coaches. What stuck out for him was the value proposition he heard. From the very first conversation, Scott heard honesty and straightforwardness. He was looking for a coach, not a friend. He wanted someone who would push him, like a good personal trainer.

A personal trainer who tells you 'great job' after two push ups is not going to help you get the results you want. He wanted someone who would be completely honest and tell him when he needed to work harder.

Scott recalls, "When I bought this business over three years ago, someone said to me, 'Oh you're the boss now. Congratulations. Today is your first day of no one ever being honest with you.' That's true. Some employees tell you what you want to hear, and sometimes I didn't know whether people were telling me the truth or not. I was looking for someone to tell me what I needed to hear, not what I wanted to hear. I wanted someone who wouldn't 'b…s…' me because that forces their credibility down and trust issues develop."

Honesty and objective feedback have been Scott's benefits of the coaching process. The company was available for takeover in part due to dysfunctional previous management, and it needed to be turned around. The employees' perspective of the way things should be done was a long way from normal. When Scott made changes, some employees insisted that the existing process was normal and that the way they were doing things was normal. He appreciated having the objective and disinterested perspective of his coach to confirm what he believed – their way was definitely not the right way. He was on the right track.

Structure was another benefit that Scott has enjoyed as a result of the coaching process. Structure helps enforce accountability, both for himself and for his employees. As the head of the company, he knew he should be focused on where the company should go, not on unproductive employees. The cycle of counseling an unproductive employee to have momentary improvement followed by a relapse was a waste of time.

"You know how the squeaky wheel gets the grease?" Scott asks. "Rather than more oil, I learned I should just get a new wheel. I learned structure from Ken, and that's one of the best things a coach can do. Structure makes you more efficient and clears your mind. Unless there's structure around something, that nagging problem can last forever and it's mentally exhausting. Structure sets you free."

He's made progress through the coaching process. His business isn't where it wants it to be, but having taken over a troubled company, it's leaps and bounds ahead of where he thought it might be at this point. The business value has increased seven-fold since he purchased the asset. As you can see, Scott is an over achiever and not yet satisfied with the growth of his company.

Coaching has also helped Scott have a healthier outlook. He admits that he had a past of holding himself responsible for things beyond his control and beating himself up for no good reason. As a baby boomer, he was of the mindset that if you weren't working 24/7, you were screwing off. Now he realizes that what he used to think of as screwing off is important self-care and is critical to make him better at what he does. He has realized that he has to empty the cup every once and a while, so he can see clearly. Leadership breakthroughs come from insights, and insights happen when the mind is relaxed. Hence Scott is at the motorcycle race track at least once a month. Scott realizes that everything that he does affects his company and distance provides perspective.

> "Structure makes you more efficient and clears your mind. Structure sets you free."
> ~ Scott S.

Scott continues, "I used to doubt myself, so Ken had me write down all of my accomplishments – every single one of them. Seeing it on paper changed my perspective. I used to have a habit of focusing on what hasn't been done. It's a bit of a 'glass half empty' concept. I'm still a perfectionist and I always want it to be better, but now I don't doubt myself. And coaching isn't just about meeting sales and company goals, it's made me a better, more well-rounded person."

Scott now uses a very structured approach: Here's the situation; here's what's needed to resolve it; here's the deadline. Freedom is the result: Freedom to move forward; freedom to appreciate accomplishments; freedom to enjoy a better quality of life.

When you look at your own situation, where are you spinning your wheels? Like Scott, is your schedule setting your agenda rather than your agenda setting your schedule. Structure will set you free, and your first freedom structure is Getting Results Coaching.

Chapter 9

Swallowed by a Whale

The bigger the corporate environment is, the harder it can be to deal with it. Like whales, big companies aren't typically agile. Then again, they don't have to be. Massive size tends to move things out of their way. Agility isn't a requirement. The bigger the company, the bigger the challenges to succeed in such an environment. Politics, inappropriate promotions, lack of credit, layers upon layers of management, ongoing confrontations and headaches. It's amazing that anything productive gets done.

Danny learned that the hard way when he went from being on staff at a company with 300 employees to being hired by one with over 100,000 employees.

"When something is that huge, that much of a leviathan—a monster, really," Danny says looking back, "it was really hard to navigate through it and very frustrating. I was getting fed up with everything and was looking for a better way to handle it. It was very stressful, and I felt like I was working my way through a Machiavellian maze, especially in my particular area. It was a very top-down organization and whenever creative or innovative ideas popped up, they were often stolen or proper credit wasn't given. It wasn't a very collegial place to work. I needed to learn new skills in this environment."

Danny knew that he needed some organization in his life in order to deal with the "monster" that was now his employer and to advance his career. Getting organized was a priority and at the suggestion of some friends, he contacted Getting Results Coaching in 2005.

Three years later, the coaching process really paid off. During the 2008-09 fiscal crisis, Danny was tasked with overseeing a crisis management desk for a particular product. He suddenly now had 14 reports, nearly all of whom were recent college graduates with no corporate experience and as raw as you could get. Additionally, they were working on three-month rotations and constantly changing as part of a graduate training program, so Danny had to develop business plans, training plans, job descriptions, meeting schedules, strategy sessions and also became the subject matter expert for senior management. It was a ton of responsibility dumped on him all at once—dumped on someone with zero prior management experience. Zip. None. Nada.

On the bright side, he was given a free enough rein to manage it the way he wanted, so he avoided the "corporate bull" and applied everything he learned as a result of his coaching work.

"At the end of the financial crisis," he recalls, "I got kudos all the way up the food chain throughout the U.S. and from our global

> "Good training is the baseline. It's how you remain calm and respond rather than react. Reacting means you don't have control. Responding means it's thought out and you can implement your plan."
> ~ Danny S.

headquarters. The coaching paid off in a way I never expected and boosted my confidence quite a bit."

Danny left the behemoth several months ago, and is now working with a group of friends, closer to home and for more money. He also credits the coaching process with improving his overall happiness. While he doesn't define himself as unhappy previously, his work with Ken opened to his eyes to see how much more happiness was possible.

Two lessons have always stuck out for Danny. First: Rice takes time to cook. He admits that that's a really big tenet for him. He's learned that patience is important and life is a process. No matter what you see on TV, there really is no instant gratification. For Danny, being able to accept and understand the process has gone a long way in his life.

His second big lesson is to stay the path. Through the coaching process, Danny shared the direction he wanted to go, and his coach helped him find the entrance to his path. Actually walking the path is something he knows he has to do alone, but a good coach is there to help self-motivate. Danny doesn't let little things distract him from his big goals.

Concentration in these two areas came home to roost for Danny in the form of Hurricane Sandy. Luckily, his challenges were limited to things like power loss and very long lines to get gas. In fact, as he moved toward the gas station a few inches at a time days after the storm, he maintained a very positive attitude.

"My life is excellent," he shares, "despite having no power. When you face a really stressful situation, it's human nature to revert to your training. Good training is the baseline. It's how you remain calm and respond rather than react. Reacting means you don't have control. Responding means it's thought out and you can implement your plan."

If there was ever a time to respond rather than react, it was in the wake and devastation of a super storm.

Danny sums it up, "Everyone goes to high school and many go on to college. A lot of folks consider that to be their development, but real development occurs when you're out in the work place and have the ability to make a difference. Hiring a coach is a big step, and a lot of people are afraid to take that step. Unfortunately, fear is a very controlling emotion, and many people let fear take control. Through coaching, I've had the opportunity to understand myself and go on to bigger and better things."

If you're feeling like you've been swallowed by a whale, whether it's navigating a professional environment or challenges in your personal life, maybe it's time to learn how you can understand yourself, change your perspective and be the person you want to be, living the life you choose.

Chapter 10

So What? Who Cares?

Worry. It's an emotion that consumes some people. Some allow worry to grind them to a halt. Worry is one of the most surefire ways to waste your precious time and energy. The worst thing about worry is that it will never deliver positive results. When you worry about that which you can't control, your only outcome will be negative – stress, anxiety, sleeplessness and possibly poor health implications as a result. Worrying about anything that you can control is equally negative. Instead, you should be using that energy to affect the outcome you desire. Asking "So what?" may be your answer.

Through coaching, Michael learned to apply "So what?" and "Who cares?" thinking. He explains, "I apply the questions 'So what?' and 'Who cares?' whenever I go through a process. For example, if I'm thinking about starting another business, I ask what might happen as a result. Maybe I'll lose the business, make a lot of money or waste my time. Asking and answering 'So what?' and 'Who cares?' helps clarify my thinking."

The reason why this helps clarify his thinking is because these questions pierce through the blanket of fear. Many people do not take action or start new ventures because they fear being embarrassed, looking foolish or experiencing pain. When we ask ourselves "So what?" we need to come up with an answer. It brings our unconscious fear to our conscious mind. Our minds do not deal well with the unknown; when we ask ourselves "So what?" it makes the unknown known.

Michael began working with Getting Results through the referral of a friend. He'd come from a background of coaching and mentoring throughout his life. When his friend suggested coaching for his business, a light bulb went on, and the driving force was his curiosity to get better.

While his business has grown and he's tripled revenues, the greatest benefit has been having a sounding board and someone to reinforce his beliefs. Coaching has helped direct him to which track he should be running on and provides a different perspective on his business.

"My level of awareness is higher," Michael says, "and working with a coach reminds me of what's important to me and brings me back to it. The process has helped me deepen relationships as well." It focuses Michael on his design and what matters to him. It is easy to get swamped in the river of Wall Street conditioning and ego.

Coaching has been an integral part of his life, and Michael has always sought out successful people as mentors including his father, athletic coaches and some managers. It surprises him when he realizes that some of his peers aren't working with a coach and are, more or less, flying by the seat of their pants.

He continues, "My coaches are a part of the team that I rely on, and that's been the biggest turning point. I'm grateful that they helped bring me to a more successful and easier way of doing things."

Although Michael has often recommended coaching, he realizes others have to be in a position to really want it. Some people have a fear of coaching or aren't willing to invest the work, money, time and energy to make a difference and improve. When others ask about how he's achieved his success, he points to coaching as the tool he uses and is a firm believer in both the process and the results.

"Learning that you're not alone on your journey is important," Michael says, "A lot of us fear being alone, especially as a business owner. Coaching helps with that psychologically, so you don't feel as if you're out there by yourself. I believe in the value of coaching."

In addition to "So what?" and "Who cares?" thinking, Michael also learned "For what?" from Ken. Whenever he'd suggest he was going to do something, the follow up question has always been "For what?". For example, if he says he's going to run a marathon, his coach prods with the "For what?" question. Many times people are choosing targets because it's the cool thing to do, or it's what they are supposed to be going after, but if you are not committed to something, the truth is you're not committed. Or if, for example, you want to make a million dollars,

> "Learning that you're not alone on your journey is important. Coaching helps with that psychologically, so you don't feel as if you're out there by yourself."
> ~ Michael S.

you coach will ask you for what? Is it for ego? Are you telling yourself the truth? It takes commitment to achieve. The "For what?" question taps into your reservoir of commitment.

When things are anchored in reality, they are much easier to achieve. If the target is real, you can hit it; if it's not real… guess what? Failure awaits. Being clear in your commitment results in developing enough reasons and justifications to go out and do it. If you aren't clear about the reason you want to do anything, success can be hit or miss. Understanding the reasons behind whatever you want to do drives motivation. Motivation delivers results especially when you are telling yourself the truth.

When you understand and are clear about the answers to "For what?" then undertaking even the greatest challenge keeps you focused and on track to succeed. Those three seemingly simple questions – So what?, Who cares? and For what? – have the potential to change your life.

Chapter 11

More Enjoyment

Working harder and harder, putting in longer and longer hours but only yielding slightly better results. Sound familiar? You've hit maximum capacity. You've reached the point of diminishing returns. The answer is not to work harder or to work longer; you no longer can. Longer days aren't paying off and may even be having the opposite effect – you're tired, burned out and now prone to mistakes… and unhappiness. Donna was at that point.

"I was no longer successful at anything," she recalls. "Not just in my business but in my personal life as well. I felt I was not succeeding in any one area at all – not my own self-satisfaction, spiritually or physically."

She saw a change in both the behavior and demeanor of a trusted colleague. He was no longer living in the calamity and chaos that typically surrounds the financial industry. Donna saw that he had become peaceful and structured. More importantly, he was more productive. She researched a number of coaches and programs before contacting Ken but found them to be too "sales-y" as she describes them.

"I used to dread coming into work," Donna continues, "because I simply hated it. I was tired going into the office every day and even more tired coming home." It seemed like there was no way out, but there was.

Through coaching, Donna learned that clients have a certain DNA-like quality, and that can be replicated to not only grow her business but to grow it into something she loves rather than something she hates. She explains, "In a coaching session, I had to do this exercise that I felt was ridiculous, and I really thought it was destined to crash and burn. I had to call my top client and say: 'I have a ridiculous request. Who would you have me meet who is like you?' And the answer I got from my client was: 'I'll get you a list.' All I had to do was ask!"

> ## "All I had to do was ask!"
> ## ~ Donna M.

Sure enough, Donna's great clients have been the path to generating similar great clients, the type of people with whom she truly enjoys working. The more she asks, the more she receives. The results have all been positive. She has reduced her total client list and now only conducts ten appointments per week instead of twenty. At the start of her career, Donna was encouraged to work 60 hours per week to develop her business, and thereafter, 40- to 50-hour work weeks were the norm. Through coaching, she's learned she doesn't have to operate that way. By learning to replicate her clients' DNA, she built the business she wanted and cut her work week to 30 hours.

Donna is now able to be very engaged with her clients. The interactions with them are now relational rather than transactional. Donna now focuses on how she can serve them rather than on what she can sell them. Her clients know they are important to her. "I choose my clients now," Donna says, "and that's not taught in this industry. I now understand that I don't have to take every client who walks through my door. I'm not Wal-Mart. A lot of advisers reach burn-out and hit a wall. That's when real frustration sets in, and I was reaching that point."

After working with a coach for only eight months, today her life is 180-degrees different. Donna is enjoying the relationships with her clients rather than hating to walk through the office door. When she hosts events, she asks her clients to each bring a friend, and they do. At a recent informational session that she offered, only 30 percent of the attendees were existing clients; the rest were friends of clients or referrals... good referrals and the type of people that match the DNA she wants in her clients.

Her reduced hours give her more time with her family, and they've noticed. There's harmony at home again. "My daughter definitely noticed," explains Donna. "She tells me, 'You're so happy, Mom and I see you more. Thank you for picking me up early. You never used to do that.' Plus I have more time to spend with my husband."

Donna hears the phrase "Aha, grasshopper, you are learning" from her coach quite a bit. It's a sign of forward progress. So is her increasing income as well as her steadily increasing client service score, a score calculated based on positive feedback from her clients. It has risen in each of the eight months in which she has been working with her coach.

Good coaching respects the learning process. Having done her research, Donna knows there are coaches and programs that she would not recommend. Good coaching is more than production or time-management coaching. It helps open your eyes and expand your understanding of your life as a whole while honoring your own values. It builds on the foundation you've already created. A good coach understands your own DNA and helps you leverage that to pave the way to the life you want to live.

Chapter 12

Reap What You Sow

Of course you reap what you sow. Why would anyone ever expect a different outcome? It's something we probably all learned in childhood, and there is no shortage of axioms that communicate that lesson: "Don't plant wheat if you need corn" or "You made your bed, now you'll have to lie in it." If you're a parent, you've probably shared similar statements with your kids. Yup. We all plant the seeds for our own outcomes.

Jeff was fully aware of that. Sowing and reaping were obviously action and consequence events. His problem wasn't that he didn't understand the concept. He wasn't planting the wrong seeds; he was having trouble getting behind the plow in the first place. Jeff was stuck in the knowing-doing gap. He knew he had potential but wasn't maximizing it. He knew what had to be done but admits he was spending too much time thinking and not enough time doing. It was a problem of spending time planning what to plant rather than actually putting the seeds in the dirt.

Jeff wasn't necessarily seeking out a coach to help him get from thinking stage to doing stage, but then Jeff met Ken. "They say sometimes you have to be at the right time and the right place," he explains, "but for me it was a matter of right time, right place, and right person."

Feeling like he had no control over his business, Jeff's frustration grew because he knew the great things he wanted to do for both his clients and the charities with which he was involved, but these important things weren't getting done. One of the lessons he learned from the coaching process was that he was the sun and whatever he shone upon would grow. With that understanding, it was time to get to work and start sowing.

The first thing he did was step back and look at what he wanted his life and career to be like. Having learned that work, home, family and spirituality are interconnected, Jeff began building his "life plan" that addressed every aspect. He continues, "Having a cohesive plan that encompasses all parts of my life put me in control rather than simply flowing with the tide."

> "Life and work are more fun because I feel more in control than before, and I'm now working toward an end result that I'm excited about."
>
> ~ Jeff W.

With his life plan in place, Jeff completed his CFP® exam and made the decision to change companies. That change not only provides better tools for him to manage accounts, it now affords him the opportunity to achieve a very important part of his "life plan" to expand his mission work in Kenya. His work with Getting Results Coaching resulted in moving from simply knowing what had to be done to actually doing it. Jeff credits the coaching process with helping him stay focused and motivated. Accountability plays a huge role in that.

"Life and work are more fun," Jeff says, "because I feel more in control than before and I'm now working toward an end result that I'm excited about." With his "life plan" in place, he's also now able to provide financial planning for individuals who have family members who are dealing with difficult issues, like Alzheimer's disease, that affect their financial outlook.

With that change, Jeff now has an assistant to whom he can delegate more work than before, freeing his time to further his missionary work. While he doesn't consider income to be a driving force for him, he has also been able to hire an assistant to help directly with the mission work, expanding what he is able to offer.

Jeff embodies Ken's quote: "You're the sun and whatever you shine upon will grow." He knew the seeds that he wanted to plant, and through coaching, he's now reaping the rewards he wanted. What areas of your life seem to be withering and failing to thrive because they lack your energy? Or like Jeff, are you spending time in the knowing-doing gap – spending too much energy on thinking and not enough on doing? With the right action, you too can become the sun and begin sowing exactly what's needed to allow you to reap the life you want.

Chapter 13

Smoother Sailing by Firing Clients

Other people are a part of life. Sure, we have people with whom we choose to spend time and whose company we enjoy and appreciate. Maybe it's a spouse or a good friend. Maybe it's even a colleague or a client. But what about those other people – the ones you must endure because of your business or your job, the ones you must endure because you have to?

You probably have some of "those other people" in your life. They're the ones who you politely try to avoid, the ones for whom you have a list of memorized excuses to end any conversation, and the ones whose number in your caller ID makes you cringe and let the call go to voice mail only to dread returning it later.

Jim had some people like that. One was a female professional acquaintance. He'd known her for years and described spending ten minutes with her as "enough." When he bumped into her at a conference, he ended up spending two hours with her – by choice. He could not believe the change in her and was shocked at the difference in her life and her perspective.

"I couldn't stop talking with her. She was a completely different person," Jim recalls. As it turned out, she'd been working with Getting Results, and the transformation Jim observed was the impetus he needed to reach out to Ken and Lauren. He worked with them for several years, took a break, and then came back again. Each time, he experienced tremendously positive results.

The coaching process helped Jim understand the importance of living life by design. He admits that he used to let his business dictate his life. He'd arrive at the office at 5:30 in the morning and typically stay fourteen hours. He had plenty of clients. In fact, he had over 1,000, and some of those clients were the type he could do without but held on to because of his preconceived notion about his business.

"Ken told me I had to fire clients," Jim explains, "and I had a fair amount of resistance to the idea. Firing clients was a pretty scary thought." With his coach's prodding, Jim started clearing his client list a little bit at a time. It became clear that it was the right thing to do. "It got to the point where I just had to jump off the cliff and trust that this approach was going to work."

It did. Jim went from having over 1,000 clients to fewer than 100, and his revenue is up four-fold. He eliminated the clients who took a lot of his time without generating results as well as those who drained his emotional capabilities. He discovered that firing clients was, in fact, very liberating rather than very scary. There are some relationships that come with a lot of baggage, both professional and personal, and by eliminating those, it creates the space needed for the really beneficial ones to expand.

"I learned that it is nearly impossible to effectively serve that many clients. At least, it is not possible to provide first class service to that many. High net worth clients expect more and deserve better service which is why I recognized the importance of cutting that number down… way down."

With that liberation, Jim also went from his 14-hour days, to spending four-day weekends on his boat every week. He shares his love of the water with a number of clients and realizes that being in alignment with clients makes it fun. "There are things you hate to do because they are work," Jim continues, "but when you set things up properly, they're not work and you don't hate them. When you do what you want, it's fun. And when you do it with who you want, it's even more fun."

The coaching process taught him to use a "what's important, what's not important" perspective, and he's applied that same principle in excising relationships that don't serve him and who he wants to be. He now works far more effectively with fewer clients, and that frees him to enjoy his life more. Relationships shouldn't be endured, they should be embraced.

At first, Jim was hesitant to share his schedule and planned time on his boat with his clients, afraid to let them know he was out of the office. He explains, "I was really surprised to learn how much my clients cared about my personal well-being and how they were willing to help me grow my business. Now they know if it's Thursday or Friday, I'm on the boat, and that doesn't bother them. They call me on my cell, or they're happy to work with my support staff. I learned that when asked correctly, they are engaged in wanting to make me successful with referrals and repeat business."

> "It got to the point where I just had to jump off the cliff and trust that this approach was going to work."
> ~ Jim D.

Through the coaching process, Jim also learned to fire without abandon when the bow is shattered and all the arrows are gone. He recalls, "We were making a presentation to a client with a $200 million potential and were up against the best national competitor. In the first few minutes, it wasn't going well and the client wasn't interested in our presentation book. At that moment, I realized the bow was broken and the arrows were gone, and I needed to dare to do something different and bold, so I closed the book, shot without abandon, and the discussion from that point went fantastically."

As of this writing, he doesn't yet know the outcome; however, he now sees that if he'd held back, the meeting would have flopped and the outcome would be destined to be negative.

Quadrupling his income by cutting his client list by 90 percent is the formula that created smooth sailing for Jim. How many clients should you fire? You probably already know their names without thinking. Imagine how you can enjoy your life without having to deal with "those other people." Why not start now?

Chapter 14

Stagnation to Success

Stagnant and stuck. Knowing you want more but not sure which way to turn to get out of the rut? When you're in a rut, it's tough to dig yourself out. Like a car stuck in a rut, you might need a push. On the other hand, some people reach a plateau. The plateau might occur after a long upward climb or possibly after a meteoric rise. You've enjoyed the ride up, but now you may be looking around from your plateau and wondering how to go up again. No matter which direction you look, it all looks the same with no place to climb. Whether it's a rut or a plateau, the end result is the same: struggling to climb out and move up again.

Annie looked at herself and realized she was growing stagnate. She'd had an admirable ride up. Born as a first-generation American of Italian parents, she overcame hurdles to advance. Culturally, women weren't allowed to do much – no college, no independence, and even learning to drive was frowned upon. Regardless, Annie set goals for herself, graduated from college, and landed a job with a broker, enjoying some success. She set a few goals and achieved them, but her career plateaued.

"Because of my upbringing, my mindset was really limiting what I could accomplish," Annie explains. "I never really saw anything higher for myself. But I witnessed a huge change in my husband who I'd known since we were twelve. He was going through the coaching process, and I saw a re-birth in him. I'll admit, I went into coaching kicking and screaming when he pointed out that I really didn't know anything about setting goals or improving my career."

Confidence was a factor. Annie didn't realize that she needed to look at herself as someone who could succeed, not just survive. The broker for whom she worked was moving up the ranks, but she never looked at what she brought to the table to make that happen. Based on her tenure of nearly 15 years, Annie figured her boss would give her what she needed and what she was entitled to, but until she took ownership of her career, it didn't happen. She needed to learn the value she provided to the team. This made a huge difference in her confidence level, her service to her clients, and her compensation rose significantly as a result.

> **"I was coached to clarify my thoughts and how to write things down effectively, so I presented what I did and what I thought I deserved in an orderly manner. It was as easy as eating ice cream."**
> **~ Annie S.**

"I was always timid about asking for money," continues Annie, "and the thought of asking for a raise would leave me hyperventilating. I was coached to clarify my thoughts and how to write things down effectively, so I presented what I did and what I thought I deserved in an orderly manner. It was as easy as eating ice cream."

When Annie followed through, creating reports that supported her work, she asked for the money she felt she deserved... and got it.

For her that was one of the biggest surprises as a result of working with Lauren of Getting Results Coaching. Annie realized she was holding herself back. Once she took ownership, the blinders and roadblocks disappeared, and Annie realized she'd been her own biggest obstacle. Through coaching, she had someone pushing her, and the relationships she had with her husband, friends, and clients blossomed.

"All my relationships grew," Annie says. "It's easy to say, 'Let's get together,' but the key is following through and doing it. I was always a great talker but failed to follow through and make it happen. My relationship with my husband is most important, and coaching has helped with that tremendously. We learned how to set goals as a couple and decide what we want to do next."

A big part of the process is becoming highly self-aware. The benefits are unique to each individual. For Annie, she got very clear that she is a nurturer at heart. The more she lived up to this role, the more fulfilled she felt. "I realized I am a born nurturer. This is a real role for me, and I needed to redesign my business to allow me to remove myself from the day to day busy-ness and free myself up to visit our clients and deepen those relationships. Aside from enjoying my time with my clients, I found that new assets flowed in easily."

In addition to volunteer work and travel, Annie and her husband teach a martial arts class for teenagers. She relishes having a part in their growth and is always left speechless when parents credit the class and her input for the incredible improvements they see in their teens.

With her relationships, career and income all growing, her quality of life blossomed as well: "My parents were factory workers, and it would break my heart to see my mom coming out of work on a hot summer's day with the factory at 130 degrees. All I ever wanted to do was take care of her. Now I can. The money I'm now earning allows me to help them with whatever they need, and I've also been able to set up college savings for my nieces and nephews. Plus Danny and I have gone from where we started in a tiny apartment to our beautiful condo."

Annie now embraces living a life by design rather than default. That's one of the most important concepts for her as a result of coaching. She's also learned the importance of having champions in her life. There are people in each of our lives who enrich our lives and make them better. It's important to take note of who in your life is adding to your well-being and who's draining it.

Although she went into the coaching process kicking and screaming, due in part to the expense, Annie now sees that it's an investment she made in herself. She viewed it as a numbers game at the start, thinking the same money could have been invested in real estate or the market with a hope of a return. However, the results she's gotten far surpass those potential gains, and Annie feels that she's quadrupled her returns by investing in herself.

How's the view from where you're standing now? Are you in a rut that you can't see out of or stuck on a plateau with no apparent way to move up again? Coaching can help you leverage the most amazing asset you have to make improvements – you! It's time to stop living your life by default.

Chapter 15

Slow Down to Grow

It's a high-speed world, and it seems to be getting faster every day and with every new iteration of technology. The faster you go, the faster you think you should go. Suddenly, top speed is no longer fast enough. You have the accelerator pressed to the floor, and life is whizzing past your window. Don't stop and don't slow down if you want to succeed is typical thinking. But that's exactly the problem – once you're at full throttle, you can't go any faster and your life is whizzing past.

Coaches weren't new to Dan. He'd worked with athletic coaches, trainers, professional coaches, and sales coaches before he came upon Ken and Getting Results Coaching. Through his life, he'd made some progress and improvements with every coach. Looking back, he sees that with some coaches, the process was either "rah-rah get motivated" to do more and work harder or it was a tactical approach, teaching him how to do more of what he was already doing. There's comes a point of diminishing return with both approaches, and Dan already had the accelerator pressed to the floor. He couldn't do more or work harder. He needed to change something, and the coaching process was the answer.

First, Dan learned to change his mindset and his approach to doing things. Think of your brain as glass of water. When it's full and you try to add more to it, it spills. The trick is to methodically dump out some of the water, allowing your brain to refill with new information.

"The movie 'The Legend of Bagger Vance' had a real impact on me," Dan says. "The idea of de-cluttering your mind to allow your natural swing to come through was a really powerful lesson. It's a matter of clearing your mind and getting rid of the clutter, so you can make it happen. This removed a lot of the frustration of running my business. It opened doors and created real freedom."

Besides de-cluttering his mind, Dan also learned the importance of de-cluttering his client list.

"I learned about the champion process," Dan explains, "to pick my top 25 clients and concentrate on them. These folks are in my 'first-class cabin' so to speak and drive most of my business."

It's the tried and true 80/20 rule in action. The majority of revenue comes from a handful of clients. However, Dan didn't select his champion list based on revenue alone. He learned it was equally critical to select those clients with whom he enjoyed working and had a really positive relationship. This selection process yielded two very positive results.

Dan continues, "It makes sense to have a champion list. I had 3,000 clients when I started the process. I couldn't give all of them what they really needed, so I was always under-delivering. By paring down the list, I now have personal relationships with my clients. With 25, now I can over-deliver and that brings with it plenty of repeat business and referrals."

The coaching process also opened Dan's eyes up to being smarter about his business. He realized that his business wasn't the end all and be all and that he used to tie his identity to his business. Now he sees his business as a tool that allows him to live the life he wants. He redesigned his business to suit his lifestyle and built it around the way he likes to work and live. Now it's a direct reflection of him and his personality, rather than the other way around – re-arranging his life to suit his business.

One of the biggest results for Dan was predictable income. There were always deals on the table that never came to fruition, and he worked on things that never offered a return. Now he does things differently.

"Cash flow was a key problem for me," Dan says, "and I'd spent tons of money trying to market to my 3,000 clients. Ultimately, that money was pretty much completely out the window. When I began focusing on my champions, I got a real ROI and steady income. The amount of effort I now have to apply to get better results is significantly less."

Plus the coaching process helped Dan realize that he needed to spend time on himself, so that he could bring a "better Dan" to both his personal and professional relationships.

> "I learned about the champion process to pick my top 25 clients and concentrate on them."
> ~ Dan N.

Dan had the pedal to the floor all day, every day. According to him, Ken was the first coach to tell him to actually slow down and give himself both permission and time to be a better person. Dan began to understand the importance of empowering selfishness in order to accomplish that.

For him, it was the biggest distinction: "When I took my foot off the gas and stopped working harder, it actually came easier. It seems counterintuitive, but when I pulled back, expansion took place."

How hard are you pressing on the accelerator? If you already have it to the proverbial floor, you can't press any harder. If you aren't getting the results you want by attempting to constantly move at high speed, it may be time to do something different. Recovery is just as important as hard training.

Chapter 16

Boredom Is Not Your Sentence

Feeling bored. It happens occasionally, but it's a huge problem when the boredom encompasses your entire life, not simply a few hours or a few days at a time. You started out with aspirations about the path your life would take: career, family, income. You've reached them. Now what? What's next? Boredom creates a vacuum, and something has to fill it. Nature abhors a vacuum, as Aristotle observed. Every space has to be filled with something, even if it is as ordinary as air. If you're not careful, it may become filled with destructive actions and behaviors.

Les learned that. He had what he describes as the perfect life: good wife, two great kids, a great job, and he was making a lot of money. But something was missing. Something didn't feel right, and he didn't have a sense of happiness. He was bored, and destructive behaviors started to creep in.

Having met Ken through a previous program, he turned to him again. Coaching offered Les a solution. "With coaching," Les explains, "I am more aware of what's going on in my head and inside me. I can recognize destructive behavior, and as importantly, I can differentiate between what's real and what might just be in my own mind. One of the beneficial coaching methods for me has been to really examine 'what story is running in my head.' It has helped me ask if this is truly what is happening or is it the story in my mind that's affecting my perspective. That has made a positive difference in the way I interact, with my team especially."

More complete awareness has been one of the real benefits Les has garnered as a result of the coaching process. A main part of that awareness is now focused on his relationships, both professional and personal, including those with his teen-aged children. He's much more aware of his clients and ultimately what they provide, and it goes even further than that.

"My relationships with my clients are much better because I go deeper with them and develop real friendships. We don't just talk business," continues Les. "I get involved in all parts of their lives. Coaching has also helped me in terms of my relationships with my kids. I notice where I would have said something before, I am able to stop and think about it first. I catch myself and ask how it would come across to them. There's a better awareness of the consequences of what comes out of my mouth."

> "My relationships with my clients are much better because I go deeper with them and develop real friendships. We don't just talk business."
> ~ Les H.

In addition to the words that he says, coaching has helped Les become more tuned in as a listener. Learned listening skills also impact his relationships. His actions can help advance those relationships, and by focusing on the concerns and wants of clients, he's learned to serve them better and be a better friend to them as well. The results are always positive.

Les sees his progress through coaching as ongoing and cites the movie "Jiro Dreams of Sushi" as a catalytic example. Jiro is an

85-year-old Sushi chef, deemed to be the world's greatest Sushi chef and a Japanese national treasure. Despite his successes, he does not believe he's reached perfection. He continues to climb to reach the top, but no one knows where the top really is. According to Jiro, "You have to love your job. You must fall in love with your work."

"There really is no reaching perfection," Les concurs. "It's not like you are going to reach perfection tomorrow and then you're done. Progress is hard to measure because it's hard to say where you are at any one time when improvement is infinite. It's a constant honing of self. There is always the potential to get better and better, and coaching has helped with that."

In addition to being cognizant of the story that may be running in his head, Les has also learned the impact of what he believes. Through the coaching process, he now believes that he is the best financial adviser and has the best wealth management team in Honolulu. The result is that his actions and the way he carries himself have changed. The way he and his team service clients has changed in order to meet that belief. Moreover, the language Les uses is no longer non-committal. "I'll try to" has been replaced with "I will." It's a small but concrete step in ensuring that things get done.

Another concept that Les embraces is that "way leads on to way." He describes it: "We are all on a certain path, and the actions that you take keep you on that path whether you're heading upward or downward. If it's downward and destructive, you won't change direction until you change your actions. I have a much greater awareness of this."

A final benefit of coaching for Les is having someone hold him accountable. According to Les, his coach doesn't mince words. "You need someone to tell you when you're making excuses or feeling sorry for yourself. I appreciate having someone to tell me like it is… besides my wife."

Are you battling boredom, having achieved much but wondering what's next? Is there a vacuum in your life that you aren't consciously filling with actions and activities that will put you on an upward path? Or like Les and Jiro, are you striving to constantly improve but unsure how to go about it? With a coach, you can eliminate the boredom in your life or learn what you need to continue on the path to progress and success.

Chapter 17

Gone Fishin'

How do you choose when there are too many choices? An extravagant buffet lets you sample a little of this and a little of that to your heart's content. That's fine when an array of choices satisfies your palate, but it's far less desirable when you are trying to run your business. When there are dozens of ways to market and dozens of ways to network, which one is best? Do you guess? Do you ask around? Like the buffet, do you try a little of this and a little of that? If that's been your approach, you probably already know it doesn't work. What worked for someone else may not be the right tack for you.

With too many choices, it's easy to get in your own way and thwart your progress. Peter faced that dilemma. He struggled with a lack of predictability. He knew what he wanted to accomplish; however, he wasn't sure which activities were the best ones to get him where he wanted to go.

Peter explains, "It's easy to be distracted by all the various things you can do in your business. There's a lot of stress, worry and anxiety over what to do. There are too many ways to try to make money, and that can hamper your ability to succeed in any one area. The biggest thing for me when I chose to work with a coach was gaining insight and confidence into the best activities for me to focus my time and marketing activities and resources on."

Based on a referral, Peter turned to Ken Doyle of Getting Results Coaching. The result is that his stress level about what he should be doing and who he should be talking to is way down, and his confidence level is way up. He no longer struggles wondering if TV ads, seminars, or personal presentations are the best ways to move his business forward. He now knows exactly who he should be talking to and what he should be focusing on. He's no longer feeling scattered. Peter learned the distinction of clarity and tenacity. Once he decided on how he was going to build his business, he stuck to it no matter what.

Building champions, Peter learned, forges better and stronger relationships with clients, and his relationships with his top clients have improved as a result of the coaching process. His best clients now know that they are not average; instead, they are in "the first class cabin."

"I looked at who I liked the most and who I wanted to grow my business with," Peter continues. "I let them know that they're special to my business and to me personally, and it was pretty awesome. They really appreciated knowing that. It's a fun way to get to know them better and also get referrals."

An avid deep-sea fisherman, Peter then took Ken's advice to invite a client to accompany him on a fishing trip. He chartered a boat for the weekend and invited one of his top clients and four of his buddies. The result was a great time, good fishing, and another new client – one that enjoys the same things Peter does.

The result was one of the things that surprised Peter the most about the coaching process: "The biggest thing about the fishing trip was having confidence that it would really work. I thought it would be fun and, on my own, would have also worried that it would be a waste of time, that no business would really result. Then I'd be faced with going back to doing things I don't like to try to drive business. But it absolutely 100 percent happens. It's like being on a high wire, and you're out there in the middle wondering if you'll make it across. A good coach ensures you that you can."

Peter's income has gone up a little, and with the tumultuous market conditions since '09, remaining even or experiencing a little growth is a positive trend, but he is also fishing and golfing at least twice a week. Although his income has not increased by as much as he would have liked, he has created more time and fun for himself. He's focused on building a business by design and one that he can truly enjoy. So Peter is growing an awesome business by doing what he loves, an approach that he never realized was a possibility until his coach showed him the way. For him, that's a much bigger benefit than income growth because he realizes the income will come. His business model is now sustainable, unlike the one he had before he took on coaching that was leading him to burnout.

> "It's like being on a high wire, and you're out there in the middle wondering if you'll make it across. A good coach ensures you that you can."
> ~ Peter M.

Business has come to Peter by doing the things he loves to do. He always tries to incorporate fishing and no longer feels guilty about spending his time on his favorite pastime. Including friends and clients increases both his enjoyment and his business at the same time.

"When I suggest coaching to others," Peter says, "the immediate question is 'How much?' and people want to know if I'm making a lot more money as a result. Money wasn't the main factor for me. Not knowing what I should be doing was a major loss of sleep. The real benefit has been the peace of mind that comes from knowing exactly what I should be doing and seeing the results. It's a bigger benefit than income. Now I can reel in a fish and still be making money, and I know that's exactly what I'm supposed to be doing. There's nothing better than that. That's being in the end zone!"

If you are in business simply to make more money, what you are really doing is being greedy and setting yourself up for failure. How can you ever hit a target called "more"? How will you know when you are making more? Play out the logic: No matter what you are doing, you can always make more money, so it's a goal that can never be achieved. And since it can never be achieved, you relieve yourself from the accountability of making a defined amount of money.

Like Peter, maybe you believe that you can't build a business by doing what you love, that your success is tied to a wide choice of activities that you don't enjoy. Because of his coach's influence, Peter has gone fishin' and is now enjoying success because of it. What's your dream job? If you believe attaining it is impossible, you're right. That perspective is exactly what's holding you back. It's time to change your thinking, so you can live the life you want to… and go fishing if you choose and make as much money as you choose to make.

Chapter 18

The Corporate Ladder Goes Nowhere

The corporate ladder – the age-old icon of professional success. At the start of your career, you stand at the bottom, look up and yearn for the top. Year by year and rung by rung you make progress. Success accompanies ascension. Another year, another rung. The problem with the corporate ladder is that climbing higher does not guarantee happiness or fulfillment. What happens when you've made progress on the ladder only to realize that your goal should have been to never climb it in the first place?

That was John's problem. He started in the industry ten years earlier and was steadily climbing. From one company to another, he continued to make progress. Another rung, more success. However, achieving success didn't bring happiness. He realized that his biggest frustration was that he was successful, very successful in fact, but not happy. Something was missing and going to work wasn't fun. The problem wasn't acute. It was gradual and chronic, so his wife and kids didn't really notice. Plus he worked to hide it from them.

John explains, "Around the dinner table every night, we'd ask, 'What was the best part of your day?' My kids and wife would answer, and it got to the point that when they asked me, I couldn't answer. I didn't have a best part of my day. So I started making stuff up. I reached the point in my frustration where I was actually lying to my kids at the dinner table.

"I really began questioning if the money was really worth it, and although I'd been fit all my life through athletics and basic training, I suddenly realized I was the heaviest I'd ever been."

> "After 15 years of that, my eyes were opened to the fact that life doesn't have to be like that, that I could accomplish certain things, do it on my own and break out of that shell. It was a complete game changer for me."
> ~ John M.

Although his growing frustration was a chronic condition, the catalyst for pursuing a coach turned out to be an acute one. John remembers the event very specifically. "There I was, climbing the ladder and making more money all the time, and there was a mid-50ish guy in my office who was doing well, at 70% of goal, had a freshman in college... and they canned him. Just like that. I suddenly realized that that could be me down the road and finally asked myself why I was putting my life and my happiness in someone else's hands."

A mutual friend told John about Getting Results and suggested he use a coach. At the time, he was 35 and realized that he'd be in his 50's before he knew it and did not want to face the same situation that his colleague did. He also realized that he couldn't wake up ten years from now doing the same thing and figured that anything's worth a three-month trial, so he called Ken.

"I wasn't his typical client," John continues. "I felt like the majority of his clients were already independent, and I was coming from corporate America. My mentality was that I had to climb the ladder, have a manager, work 9:00 to 5:00, and fit the corporate cultural mold. After 15 years of that, my eyes were opened to the fact that life doesn't have to be like that, that I could accomplish certain things, do it on my own and break out of that shell. It was a complete game changer for me."

Game changer, indeed. Although he had a big mortgage and three young kids, John decided to cut his ties with the corporate world and take the leap to go it on his own. He flipped his life 180 degrees. He didn't take any clients and started from scratch, risking his house and possibly some of his relationships. But the idea of living life by design was what had been missing for him. It came with a financial price: John started by making fifty percent less. However, there's also a huge upside.

He now gets up with more energy every day with ownership of his business and his life. His commute to the office is now five minutes rather than an hour and a half. One of the best things is that he no longer has to lie at the dinner table. "Now when they ask me about the best part of my day, I can say, 'I helped somebody retire today. I helped somebody with their money today and they have a better life. I went to your soccer game today.' I call all the shots now. While I'm making half of what I did, I know that in two or three years, I could easily be making much, much more than I was when I left the corporate world. The crazy part is that 90% of the country would take my old salary in a minute, but I could not be happy continuing on that path."

John credits the coaching process with his choice to take the chance he did and develop it successfully. He has many friends who are on the same track he was and can't fathom taking the leap that he did. They all agree that if they could they would. The reality is they can. Everyone who knows John knows he's working with a coach, and he recommends the process. "I am the poster child for what can be accomplished with a coach," he shares. "It's an investment and you can't measure it tit-for-tat the way that some people want to. It's hard to quantify, and the final chapters have yet to be written."

Clearly, John is now living his life by design – by his own design, and he credits the coaching process with getting him off the ladder to realize and embrace what his life could really be like. Are you measuring your own success by your ascent up the ladder? If so, is it really working for you? Or is looking up the ladder doing nothing more than giving you a stiff neck? Do you look out from your place on the ladder and see the place where you'd really rather be? It is possible and you can live the life you envision.

Chapter 19

Be Careful What You Ask For

Being micromanaged. Lacking concrete direction for advancement. Not getting credit for the work you accomplish, or worse, having someone else take that credit. Limited or nonexistent exposure and opportunity for advancement. These complaints are all too common in the corporate workplace, and these complaints were at the top of Patrick's list. Add to that stagnation in his career and feeling like the purpose in his work wasn't being achieved. He knew he needed to go outside of his comfort zone, and he needed help to do so.

"I had risen to a level just below partner," Patrick recalls, "and I was in line for a partnership in my accounting area of specialty. When I began making detailed inquiries about the requirements to move to the next level, the company wouldn't commit to a formal plan to allow me to develop. I felt like I was left high and dry without concrete answers about what I needed to do to reach the next level, and that was not acceptable."

His solution was to seek out a coach, and through the recommendation of a friend, Patrick contacted Lauren at Getting Results. He knows that he was underdeveloped and not challenged enough, nor was he getting the exposure he needed to move to the next level. Cruising on Easy Street, he had plenty of time to develop networking skills and contacts, but he knew he wasn't doing enough.

As it turns out, one of his contacts paid off, and paid off handsomely. As a result of the design he chose, he signed on with another firm that focused on his area of accounting specialty. "Through the process, I was coached on how to cultivate key relationships," explains Patrick. "As a result, I was offered a new position that addressed the stagnation and underdevelopment I felt. It was a direct answer to all of the problems I was having and afforded me many more opportunities immediately. I went from zero to sixty in an instant! Be careful what you ask for because you just might get it. And I got exactly what I asked for. I got it all exactly as I wanted, and it is the most unbelievable challenge of my professional life."

The first step was getting the salary he wanted. He suggested his top number as his initial salary request, and the company granted it. Conversation over; no need for negotiation. Patrick credits what he learned through coaching to use the right language from the start. He learned how to properly value himself. Additionally, his confidence was high, allowing him to sell himself high. Chalk it up to another benefit of having a coach.

Patrick continues, "I'm in a new league. It's a different ballgame than before, and it's the big leagues now. Professionally, I set myself up to go even further in my career. My reputation and stature are increasing, and my reputation in the industry continues to grow. I have signed on with a winner."

When he started the process, he had no idea how he was going to achieve his objectives. This is often where so many people get stuck or stopped in their quest for success. They try to figure the 'how,' and when they can't see how they will accomplish it, they give up before they ever get started.

Patrick is also learning through coaching that the work has to focus on what's going on inside of him rather than outside of him. He admits he's been spending too much time and energy trying to change what's outside and is working now to focus on changing himself inside instead, moving from a perception of victimhood to one of autonomy over his life. He's learning that life never gives you more than you can handle and adaptation is the key to success. "I contacted Lauren to open my life. Be careful what you ask for…." he repeats with a hearty laugh.

The coaching exercise that has had a most profound impact on him has been to create a collage of images – images that reflect what he wants his life to look like. He searched the Internet and downloaded about 25 images. One that is central to his collage is that of a businessman on the corner of 42nd and Park with his hands in the air. Patrick sees himself in this image by closing the massive deal that is his new position. Additionally, he sees

> "It made my goals feel tangible instead of just a nice thought."
> ~ Patrick H.

that many of his selected images reflect his relationship with his life partner in social settings that combine work and pleasure. He explains, "The impact and power that this exercise has had on my life is ridiculous. It turned my life upside down, and in a great way. Visualizing this has had a huge impact. It made my goals feel tangible instead of just a nice thought." This was critical since he had some very lofty goals.

His acquaintances can easily look to Patrick as an example of reaping the benefits of coaching. "I think that it takes a lot of courage to make a pro-active choice to ask for help," Patrick concludes. "I say that because when I do it (ask for help), I feel a sense of inadequacy that I don't already know something, and, therefore, I need to ask for help. There's courage needed in standing up to those feelings…

standing up to the feelings and taking the risk to do it anyway." Had he allowed his insecurity to take over, he would never be in the place he is today. His coach credits Patrick's coach-ability and willingness to follow through on whatever she threw at him to his success.

What is it you would like to ask for in your career and your life? Where are your stagnations and what is keeping you from the next level? Through coaching, you can define them and overcome them. Like Patrick, you may find yourself going from zero to sixty, living a life by design rather than accepting a life by default.

Chapter 20

A Compass and a Map

A compass and a map are great tools, but one without the other can be pretty useless. A compass alone will point you in a specific direction, but without a map, how will you know if the direction you choose is the right one? On the other hand, a map provides a wealth of information, but if you don't know which way you're headed, you'll only reach your destination by sheer luck or probably not without making a lot of wrong turns along the way. Maybe you're like Jon: He knew what he wanted but he had no plan in place to get it and admits he was winging it.

Are you dreaming of a nice home, more money, a once-in-a-lifetime trip, success, happiness? Possibly you've even taken the step to write down goals like those. Great. You have a compass. You know where you want to go, but if you start your journey without a map, you're winging it like Jon was. Moving without knowing which way you're headed and making wrong turns are frustrating time-wasters. Jon knew that. He had plenty of experience with it.

"I had my goals," Jon says, "but I had no plan and no accountability. It was frustrating. I would grow a bit, but then I'd plateau. There were extreme highs, but also a lot of extreme lows. I was working long hours and not seeing my family. I worked weekends to try to get my business where I wanted it to go. I always figured that the harder I worked, the more money I could make. I was always trying to drum up business, but that left no time for my family or the things I liked to do."

Jon didn't really have a map, and he knew it. Then his partner referred him to Getting Results Coaching. That was in the mid-90's when the market was great and it was easy to do business. Easy that is until the tech bubble burst. Since it was easy Jon saw no reason to take on coaching. Why change when you are getting good results? Good results were the root of the inaction because they could have been outstanding results. The financial industry brings with it a delusional culture of speed. The markets move fast, so decisions have to be quick and results even quicker. Jon realized things weren't really working for him, and he and his partner were guilty of the instant gratification mind-set. Before either of them began the coaching process, they'd try different projects and shelve them if the results weren't immediate.

Now Jon has a much different perspective. "It's like cooking rice," he continues, "it takes time. I've learned that I have to stick with things and eliminate immediate gratification thinking."

> "I've learned that I have to stick with things and eliminate immediate gratification thinking."
> ~ Jon T.

All things of value take time and attention. You need to be clear on where you are on your proverbial map and where you are going. Success is moving one deliberate step at a time in the clear direction of your design.

Jon also credits the coaching process with increasing his overall awareness. He's now very aware of how he's being. Previously, he would get frustrated and stew for a few days, thinking "This isn't working. This is hard." While he still gets frustrated at times, he now sees the emotion clearly and asks if it's advantageous. He no longer carries the frustration with him. Instead, he acknowledges it and keeps moving forward.

Jon explains, "Before coaching, events would erupt at work or at home and it skewed my attention. Now I am able to accept things that happen and develop Plan B. I no longer waste time with regret and worrying that things are hard or will take too much time. It's a lot like a golfer fine tuning his swing. It's a little adjustment here or a little tweak there, and I'm back in the game. The weekly sessions provide the small changes I need to stay on track, and it keeps me accountable."

Jon has also learned a lot about income. He grew up watching his parents work long and hard to make ends meet, and prior to coaching, he was convinced that everything was tied to production. Everything hinged on what he could and would produce. Now he sees that his income is derived from what he can do for his clients, family, friends and his community. His income level is no longer tied to how hard he works, and that's the biggest surprise for him. The less he works, the more he can do and the more money he can make. It is one of the counter intuitive principles of Getting Results Coaching.

As a result of the coaching process, his practice has quadrupled in asset size. Jon describes it: "My practice is built on people I love and they love me. We love to work together. My income is now linked to what I give back to people. I enjoy helping people, and my income grows that way. That approach has given me the financial freedom to provide for my kids the way I want to, to live in the neighborhood of my dreams, and to help family, friends and organizations with time as well as money."

What Jon offers his clients goes well beyond financial advice. He delves into the lives of his clients whether it's to follow up on their grandchildren or discuss a recent vacation and where they want to go next. When people use the phrase "I wish I could," Jon finds the resource or solution to answer that.

"Through coaching, Ken made me identify what I've been put here on Earth to do," Jon says. "And that is to create space in people's lives to let their wishes and dreams come to fruition. I help people do what they want to do. Sometimes I look back and think that I can't believe I'm able to do all this and not get burned out by it. It's growing and it's in alignment with my life, so it naturally all fits in."

Jon's proverbial compass and map keep him on track to fulfill not only his own dreams, but those of many of his clients as well. Where are you in your life now? If you aren't sure or if you don't know how to get where you want to go, a compass and a map are definitely in order.

Chapter 21

Business by Design

Helene does not live in an 'OR' world. She lives in an 'AND' world. She can be a great mom AND a successful business woman AND live a life by design. Most people limit themselves based on generic programming. Traditional programming says that in order to be successful, you have to be the first in the office and the last to leave, often at the sacrifice of other areas including your family, health, and passions.

To most of Helene's colleagues, she looked like an enigma (a word often used to describe individuals who have been through the program). As a producing advisor, she became and maintained her status as a Million Dollar Producer while working from 10:00 a.m.to 2:00 p.m., hours that anybody would dream of, let alone someone at that high level.

Her coaches would all tell you that Helene is very coachable. She does the work and reaps the rewards.

Helene is no stranger to coaching and sits on both sides of the desk, so to speak. She's been coached for years by Ken and Lauren and by their predecessors before that. "I've been using coaches my whole life," Helene recalls. "We've worked together for so many years and in so many ways. I've wanted to learn as much as I could to enhance my life and get clear on all the different pieces of my life in which I could improve. Working with coaches helped me get really clear on what I needed to do to always take my life to the next level."

The overall benefits and positive impact of using a coach are certainly underscored when a coach chooses to be coached. Maybe you find that surprising or are scratching your head, wondering why. There are two simple reasons: accountability and objectivity. Very rare are the individuals who can push themselves with the level of self-discipline needed to persevere when the going gets tough, really tough. We're all pretty good at letting ourselves off the hook. You may shake your head and convince yourself that you do have the self-discipline you need to achieve your higher goals in life. And you may be right. Maybe.

First came efficiency improvement. Helene applied her experience and the coaching concepts she learned to create as many efficiencies in her business as possible. That results in a four-hour work day. "I got very clear on the things I didn't want to do and the things I like to do," continues Helene. "For the things I didn't want to do, I created systems so I could teach others and delegate the work to them. A good coach helps you do that. I worked to deepen my relationships with clients more efficiently rather than by spending more time on it. That's time I would rather spend with my family. Through coaching, I was able to deepen relationships that are key to a successful business without doing things I didn't really enjoy."

Efficiency allows Helene to focus on the parts of her business that she enjoys and on relationship building. She's excised the administrative aspect of her business from her day, knowing her time is better spent elsewhere. That has freed her for a much higher quality of life, including focusing on one of her passions – building a career planning business designed for college students.

She recognizes the benefit of accountability and that without it, it's hard to make a lot of things happen. Helene has always appreciated the exercises and challenges that forced her to look at herself to determine what she really wanted to accomplish. The coaching process has allowed the results to happen more efficiently, effectively and at all.

That's where the second benefit of coaching comes in: objectivity. Even the most self-disciplined among us is limited by perspective. We're all limited to see the world around us through our own eyes and by our own perceptions. Another set of eyes to look at any problem or challenge we face is invaluable. A different perspective and a different set of experiences is often the key to finding the right solution. It goes back to the adage, "Two heads are better than one."

> "I worked to deepen my relationships with clients more efficiently rather than by spending more time on it. That's time I would rather spend with my family."
> ~ Helene N.

Most recently, Helene worked with Lauren to help develop her idea into a small business and to ultimately grow that small business into a big, successful business. She explains, "I needed a lot of help getting organized and prioritized to know what the key steps are that I need to take – one in front of the other, in front of the other. I'm a big-picture type person, so it's hard for me to sometimes see the small, but very necessary, steps that are needed. Working with a coach, we broke it down and put it in order. For example, with coaching, I could itemize what three things had to be done this week in order to move the process to the next step. I need a guide to support me along the way and bring me back when I get off track."

It was first a matter of objectivity – help seeing what had to be done, followed by accountability – knowing there would be someone to whom she had to report the following week with the progress.

One of Helene's initial goals was to double her income. With that accomplished, she focuses on others areas in which she has a strong interest. In working with her coaches, she's developed much deeper relationships and learned a different way to approach her business. Like so many others, she took apart her business and found the people she liked, the people with whom she wanted to surround herself. She worked hard to intensify her rapport with those people, and the result was a business that was both more fun and more profitable.

"One of the great values of coaching," says Helene, "is uncovering the blind spots that I've had or that any person would have. Life is really about living to your highest potential. I want that for myself and for the kids I coach. My calling in life is to help college kids live their dream job. That is naturally what I look to do. Whatever I can't see for myself, my coach gives me another set of eyes. We all get caught in the blind spots that we don't know we have and that are hampering us. We're all subjective people! Coaching provides objectivity, and I'm constantly uncovering the blind spots that may be hindering me from moving forward."

Coaching provides a safe and non-judgmental environment to explore dreams and aspirations and the obstacles that may prevent their achievement. Helene experiences that both as a "coachee" and a coach herself. There are always some people with a certain resistance to coaching, but when Helene sees people struggling, either financially or with other aspects of their lives, she listens carefully to what the real road blocks are.

"I try to uncover what they're not feeling great about, and gently suggest they try coaching once," concludes Helene. "I try to meet the person where they are and understand their disappointment. 'Financial? Business growth? Organizational or client issues? I have the greatest solution for you!' I'd always like them to at least try it and see if they feel an alignment and connection with coaching. 'Give it a try. What do you have to lose? There truly is no downside.' I know people will always get a few pearls from any coaching conversation that will move something positively forward for them."

It's that simple: What do you have to lose? If you're struggling with any aspect in your life, that struggle is already a negative impact and is impairing your ability to enjoy the quality of life you deserve. If you are struggling, the things you may have tried to correct it are obviously not working... or you wouldn't still be struggling. Coaching provides the accountability and objectivity you probably need to put you on the right path. Isn't your happiness and fulfillment in life worth a small investment of your time and money? Only you hold the answer to that question.

The Next Step

Having read the stories of these individuals who changed their lives and achieved what they set out to accomplish, we're hoping you've been inspired! Quite possibly you saw yourself in one or more of their stories, facing similar struggles with similar aspirations.

We're also hoping that you've gained a few bits of wisdom through their words and what they've learned. No doubt you picked up on common threads that run through their experiences: Live life by design, not default. Take responsibility for your outcomes and be accountable rather than play the victim. There's a difference between being busy and being productive. Divest yourself of the business and personal relationships that aren't benefitting you and embrace those that are. Commit to professional development by hiring a guide or a coach.

While you likely found that there were common themes in many of the lessons they've learned, the application of their knowledge is as individual as each of these people. The same is true for you. You're unique, and that uniqueness is at the heart of your road to success. Sure, you could read this book over and read any of the tens of thousands of business development books available (and your bookshelf may already be lined with many of them), but working with someone who understands you and who is there to personally help you find your path is more valuable than any book. The challenge with just reading books is that you are still processing the information given through the same, unchanged filter that often leads to the same results. Working with someone like a coach helps you alter the filters to effectively create lasting change in your business as well as your life.

Take a moment to reflect on where you are in your business at this moment. Are you in a rut or on a treadmill? Is your business doing what it is supposed to do (i.e. producing enough money for you to live exactly the way that you choose to live)? Or are you stuck in the "knowing-doing" gap – you know what you need to do but can't seem to get around to doing it? I submit that if you believe you know what to do but aren't doing it, then you really don't know what to do! Don't be fooled. Is your day running you rather than the other way around? Are you trying to please everyone, and in turn, pleasing no one? Are you unclear as to where your next deal is coming from? Do you want to move your business forward but aren't sure how to go about it? Are you mired in worry and regret? Would you like to rejuvenate your enthusiasm for your work... and your life?

Learning doesn't end with the formal education of high school and college. In fact, with more life experiences under your belt, your ability to learn and apply knowledge increases. The right coach will help you learn, but more importantly, you will gain a fresh perspective and new ways to look at and overcome old and ongoing challenges.

It's simple: In all facets of sports and life, the best of the best use coaches. Those at the pinnacle got there with the help of a coach. You've probably made a number of investments throughout your life. Your most lucrative investment would be in the very asset you control: yourself and your business. Like those who told their stories, you will find that the results will provide the greatest return on any investment you ever made.

Why do some people in your business make multiples of the income that you do? How can someone in Financial Services make one million in a year while you make $200k, making five times as much as you? Can someone in your profession really be five times smarter than you, five times better looking, or five times more motivated than you are? As a matter of fact, in human performance, there are no multipliers. There is one field where people can outperform you by a factor of five or ten. That is in business. You probably know some people in your firm who are out-producing you by five, seven or even ten times. You work as hard as they do! In fact, you are smarter and better looking than they are, yet they still out produce you!

The only difference between you and the advisor that is out-producing you by five times is that they have a slight edge. Each of the individuals whose stories you have read has developed their slight individual edges. The most successful people you know in the industry are not that different from you. They all get up in the morning and put one pant leg on at a time and pee after drinking three cups of coffee. So why are they out-producing you by so much?

I promise that you will be very surprised at what an eye-opening experience a fresh perspective can be and how the slight edge can produce incredible results. You'll be amazed at what you can accomplish when you're truly held accountable.

We'd like to leave you with two questions: What is it that you want your business to do for your life? What will you do to alter its current trajectory?

It takes new action to get new results. Stop reading and take action!

Take the next step and learn more at www.FinancialAdvisorCoach. com. You have nothing to lose and everything to gain.

www.ingramcontent.com/pod-product-compliance
Lightning Source LLC
Chambersburg PA
CBHW051219170526

45166CB00005B/1963